FOUR ESSAYS

MICHEL
DE MONTAIGNE

FOUR ESSAYS

Translated by M. A. Screech

penguin books

PENGUIN BOOKS

Published by the Penguin Group

Penguin Books USA Inc., 375 Hudson Street,
New York, New York 10014, U.S.A.

Penguin Books Ltd, 27 Wrights Lane, London W8 5TZ, England

Penguin Books Australia Ltd, Ringwood, Victoria, Australia

Penguin Books Canada Ltd, 10 Alcorn Avenue,
Toronto, Ontario, Canada M4V 3B2

Penguin Books (N.Z.) Ltd, 182–190 Wairau Road,
Auckland 10, New Zealand

Penguin Books Ltd, Registered Offices:
Harmondsworth, Middlesex, England

These essays are taken from *The Complete Essays* by Michel de
Montaigne, translated by M. A. Screech, published by Penguin Books.
This edition published 1995.

CONTENTS

FOUR ESSAYS

On the Cannibals

[*The cannibals mentioned in this chapter lived on the coasts of Brazil. Montaigne had read many accounts of the conquest of the New World, including Girolamo Benzoni's* Historia del mondo novo *(Venice, 1565) in the French translation by Urbain Chauveton, the very title of which emphasizes the dreadful treatment of the natives by the Conquistadores:* A New History of the New World containing all that Spaniards have done up to the present in the West Indies, and the harsh treatment which they have meted out to those people yonder ... Together with a short History of a Massacre committed by the Spaniards on some Frenchmen in Florida *(two editions in 1579).*

Montaigne's 'primitivism' (his respect for barbarous peoples and his admiration for much of their conduct, once their motives are understood) has little in common with the 'noble savages' of later centuries. These people are indeed cruel: but so are we. Their simple ways have much to teach us: they can serve as a standard by which we can judge Plato's Republic, the myth of the Golden Age, the cruelty, the corruption and the culture of Europe, and show up that European insularity which condemns peoples as barbarous merely because their manners and their dress are different.]

When King Pyrrhus crossed into Italy, after noting the excellent formation of the army which the Romans had sent ahead towards him he said, 'I do not know what kind of Barbarians these are' (for the Greeks called all foreigners Barbarians) 'but there is nothing barbarous about the ordering of the army which I can see!' The Greeks said the same about the army which Flaminius brought over to their country, as did Philip when he saw from a hill-top in his kingdom the order and plan of the Roman encampment under Publius Sulpicius Galba.[1] We should be similarly wary of accepting common opinions; we should judge them by the ways of reason not by popular vote.

I have long had a man with me who stayed some ten or twelve years in that other world which was discovered in our century when Villegaignon made his landfall and named it *La France Antartique*.[2] This discovery of a boundless territory seems to me worthy of reflection. I am by no means sure that some other land may not be discovered in the future, since so many persons, greater than we are, were wrong about this one! I fear that our eyes are bigger than our bellies, our curiosity more[3] than

1. Plutarch, *Life of Pyrrhus* and *Life of Flaminius*.

2. Durand de Villegaignon struck land, in Brazil, in 1557. Cf. *Lettres sur la navigation du chevalier de Villegaignon es terres de l'Amérique*, Paris, 1557, by an author who calls himself simply N.B.

3. '80: our bellies, *as they say, applying it to those whose appetite and hunger make them desire more meat than they can manage: I fear that we too have* curiosity *far* more . . .

we can stomach. We grasp at everything but clasp nothing but wind.

Plato brings in Solon to relate that he had learned from the priests of the town of Saïs in Egypt how, long ago before the Flood, there was a vast island called Atlantis right at the mouth of the Straits of Gibraltar, occupying an area greater than Asia and Africa combined; the kings of that country, who not only possessed that island but had spread on to the mainland across the breadth of Africa as far as Egypt and the length of Europe as far as Tuscany, planned to stride over into Asia and subdue all the peoples bordering on the Mediterranean as far as the Black Sea. To this end they had traversed Spain, Gaul and Italy and had reached as far as Greece when the Athenians withstood them; but soon afterwards those Athenians, as well as the people of Atlantis and their island, were engulfed in that Flood.[4]

It is most likely that that vast inundation should have produced strange changes to the inhabitable areas of the world; it is maintained that it was then that the sea cut off Sicily from Italy –

> *Hæc loca, vi quondam et vasta convulsa ruina,*
> *Dissiluisse ferunt, cum protinus utraque tellus*
> *Una foret.*

4. Plato, *Timaeus*, 24E etc., and Girolamo Benzoni, *Historia del mondo novo*, Venice 1565. Cf. also Plato, *Critias*, 113 A ff.

[Those places, they say, were once wrenched apart by a violent convulsion, whereas they had formerly been one single land.][5]

– as well as Cyprus from Syria, and the island of Negropontus from the Boeotian mainland, while elsewhere lands once separated were joined together by filling in the trenches between them with mud and sand:

> *sterilisque diu palus aptaque remis*
> *Vicinas urbes alit, et grave sentit aratrum*

[Barren swamps which you could row a boat through now feed neighbouring cities and bear the heavy plough.][6]

Yet there is little likelihood of that island's being the New World which we have recently discovered, for it was virtually touching Spain; it would be unbelievable for a flood to force it back more than twelve hundred leagues to where it is now; besides our modern seamen have already all but discovered that it is not an island at all but a mainland, contiguous on one side with the East Indies and on others with lands lying beneath both the Poles – or that if it is separated from them, it is by straits so narrow

5. Virgil, *Aeneid*, III, 414–17.
6. Horace, *Ars poetica*, 65–6.

that it does not deserve the name of 'island' on that account.

It seems that large bodies such as these are subject, as are our own, to changes, some natural, some feverish.[7] When I consider how my local river the Dordogne has, during my own lifetime, been encroaching on the right-hand bank going downstream and has taken over so much land that it has robbed many buildings of their foundation, I realize that it has been suffering from some unusual upset: for if it had always gone on like this or were to do so in the future, the whole face of the world would be distorted. But their moods change: sometimes they incline one way, then another: and sometimes they restrain themselves. I am not discussing those sudden floodings whose causes we know. By the coast-line in Médoc, my brother the Sieur d'Arsac can see lands of his lying buried under sand spewed up by the sea: the tops of some of the buildings are still visible: his rents and arable fields have been changed into very sparse grazing. The locals say that the sea has been thrusting so hard against them for some time now that they have lost four leagues of land. These sands are the sea's pioneer-corps: and we can see those huge shifting sand-dunes marching a half-league ahead in the vanguard, capturing territory.

7. '88: changes *sickly* and feverish. When . . .

The other testimony from Antiquity which some would make relevant to this discovery is in Aristotle – if that little book about unheard wonders is really his.[8] He tells how some Carthaginians struck out across the Atlantic beyond the Straits of Gibraltar, sailed for a long time and finally discovered a large fertile island entirely clothed in woodlands and watered by great deep rivers but very far from any mainland; they and others after them, attracted by the richness and fertility of the soil, emigrated with their wives and children and started living there. The Carthaginian lords, seeing that their country was being gradually depopulated, expressly forbade any more to go there on pain of death and drove out those new settlers, fearing it is said that they would in time increase so greatly that they would supplant them and bring down their State.

But that account in Aristotle cannot apply to these new lands either.

That man of mine was a simple, rough fellow – qualities which make for a good witness: those clever chaps notice more things more carefully but are always adding glosses; they cannot help changing their story a little in order to make their views triumph and be more persuasive; they

8. The *Secreta secretorum* is supposititious. Montaigne is following Girolamo Benzoni.

never show you anything purely as it is: they bend it and disguise it to fit in with their own views. To make their judgement more credible and to win you over they emphasize their own side, amplify it and extend it. So you need either a very trustworthy man or else a man so simple that he has nothing in him on which to build such false discoveries or make them plausible; and he must be wedded to no cause. Such was my man; moreover on various occasions he showed me several seamen and merchants whom he knew on that voyage. So I am content with what he told me, without inquiring what the cosmographers have to say about it.

What we need is topographers who would make detailed accounts of the places which they had actually been to. But because they have the advantage of visiting Palestine, they want to enjoy the right of telling us tales about all the rest of the world! I wish everyone would write only about what he knows – not in this matter only but in all others. A man may well have detailed knowledge or experience of the nature of one particular river or stream, yet about all the others he knows only what everyone else does; but in order to trot out his little scrap of knowledge he will write a book on the whole of physics! From this vice many great inconveniences arise.

Now to get back to the subject, I find (from what has been told me) that there is nothing savage or barbarous about those peoples, but that every man calls barbarous anything he is not accustomed to; it is indeed the case that we have no other criterion of truth or right-reason than the example and form of the opinions and customs of our own country. There we always find the perfect religion, the perfect polity, the most developed and perfect way of doing anything! Those 'savages' are only wild in the sense that we call fruits wild when they are produced by Nature in her ordinary course: whereas it is fruit which we have artificially perverted and misled from the common order which we ought to call savage. It is in the first kind that we find their true, vigorous, living, most natural and most useful properties and virtues, which we have bastardized in the other kind by merely adapting them to our corrupt tastes. Moreover, there is a delicious savour which even our taste finds excellent in a variety of fruits produced in those countries without cultivation: they rival our own. It is not sensible that artifice should be reverenced more than Nature, our great and powerful Mother. We have so overloaded the richness and beauty of her products by our own ingenuity that we have smothered her entirely. Yet wherever her pure light does shine, she wondrously shames our vain and frivolous enterprises:

> *Et veniunt ederæ sponte sua melius,*
> *Surgit et in solis formosior arbutus antris,*

Et volucres nulla dulcius arte canunt.

[Ivy grows best when left untended; the strawberry tree
flourishes more beautifully in lonely grottoes, and
birds sing the sweeter for their artlessness.][9]

All our strivings cannot even manage to reproduce the
nest of the smallest little bird, with its beauty and appropri-
ateness to its purpose; we cannot even reproduce the web
of the wretched spider. Plato says that all things are
produced by nature, fortune or art, the greatest and fairest
by the first two, the lesser and least perfect by the last.[10]

Those peoples, then, seem to me to be barbarous only
in that they have been hardly fashioned by the mind of
man, still remaining close neighbours to their original
state of nature. They are still governed by the laws of
Nature and are only very slightly bastardized by ours; but
their purity is such that I am sometimes seized with
irritation at their not having been discovered earlier, in
times when there were men who could have appreciated
them better than we do. It irritates me that neither
Lycurgus nor Plato had any knowledge of them, for it
seems to me that what experience has taught us about
those peoples surpasses not only all the descriptions with

9. Propertius, I, ii, 10–12.
10. Plato, *Laws*, X, 888A–B.

which poetry has beautifully painted the Age of Gold[11] and all its ingenious fictions about Man's blessed early state, but also the very conceptions and yearnings of philosophy. They could not even imagine a state of nature so simple and so pure as the one we have learned about from experience; they could not even believe that societies of men could be maintained with so little artifice, so little in the way of human solder. I would tell Plato that those people have no trade of any kind, no acquaintance with writing, no knowledge of numbers, no terms for governor or political superior, no practice of subordination or of riches or poverty, no contracts, no inheritances, no divided estates, no occupation but leisure, no concern for kinship – except such as is common to them all – no clothing, no agriculture, no metals, no use of wine or corn. Among them you hear no words for treachery, lying, cheating, avarice, envy, backbiting or forgiveness. How remote from such perfection would Plato find that Republic which he thought up *'viri a diis recentes'* [men fresh from the gods].[12]

11. Cf. Elizabeth Armstrong, *Ronsard and the Age of Gold*, Cambridge, 1968.

12. Seneca, *Epist. moral.*, XC, 44. (This epistle is a major defence of the innocence of natural man before he was corrupted by philosophy and progress.)

Hos natura modos primum dedit.

[These are the ways which Nature first ordained.][13]

In addition they inhabit a land with a most delightful countryside and a temperate climate, so that, from what I have been told by my sources, it is rare to find anyone ill there;[14] I have been assured that they never saw a single man bent with age, toothless, bleary-eyed or tottering. They dwell along the sea-shore, shut in to landwards by great lofty mountains, on a stretch of land some hundred leagues in width. They have fish and flesh in abundance which bear no resemblance to ours; these they eat simply cooked. They were so horror-struck by the first man who brought a horse there and rode it that they killed him with their arrows before they could recognize him, even though he had had dealings with them on several previous voyages. Their dwellings are immensely long, big enough to hold two or three hundred souls; they are covered with the bark of tall trees which are fixed into the earth, leaning against each other in support at the top, like some of our barns where the cladding reaches down to the ground and

13. Virgil, *Georgics*, II, 208.
14. One of Montaigne's sources was Simon Goulart's *Histoire du Portugal*, Paris, 1587, based on a work by Bishop Jeronimo Osorio (da Fonseca) and others.

acts as a side. They have a kind of wood so hard that they use it to cut with, making their swords from it as well as grills to cook their meat. Their beds are woven from cotton and slung from the roof like hammocks on our ships; each has his own, since wives sleep apart from their husbands. They get up at sunrise and have their meal for the day as soon as they do so; they have no other meal but that one. They drink nothing with it, like those Eastern peoples who, according to Suidas,[15] only drink apart from meals. They drink together several times a day, and plenty of it. This drink is made from a certain root and has the colour of our claret. They always drink it lukewarm; it only keeps for two or three days; it tastes a bit sharp, is in no ways heady and is good for the stomach; for those who are not used to it it is laxative but for those who are, it is a very pleasant drink. Instead of bread they use a certain white product resembling coriander-cakes. I have tried some: it tastes sweet and somewhat insipid.

They spend the whole day dancing; the younger men go off hunting with bow and arrow. Meanwhile some of the women-folk are occupied in warming up their drink: that is their main task. In the morning, before their meal,

15. Suidas, *Historica, caeteraque omnia quae ad cognitionem rerum spectant*, Basle, 1564.

one of their elders walks from one end of the building to the other, addressing the whole barnful of them by repeating one single phrase over and over again until he has made the rounds, their building being a good hundred yards long. He preaches two things only: bravery before their enemies and love for their wives. They never fail to stress this second duty, repeating that it is their wives who season their drink and keep it warm. In my own house, as in many other places, you can see the style of their beds and rope-work as well as their wooden swords and the wooden bracelets with which they arm their wrists in battle, and the big open-ended canes to the sound of which they maintain the rhythm of their dances. They shave off all their hair, cutting it more cleanly than we do, yet with razors made of only wood or stone. They believe in the immortality of the soul: souls which deserve well of the gods dwell in the sky where the sun rises; souls which are accursed dwell where it sets. They have some priests and prophets or other, but they rarely appear among the people since they live in the mountains. When they do appear they hold a great festival and a solemn meeting of several villages – each of the barns which I have described constituting a village situated about one French league distant from the next. The prophet then addresses them in public, exhorting them to be virtuous and dutiful, but their entire system of ethics contains only the same 13 two articles: resoluteness in battle and love for their wives. He foretells what is to happen and the results they must expect from what they undertake; he either incites them to war or deflects them from it, but only on condition that if he fails to divine correctly and if things turn out other than he foretold, then – if they can catch him – he is condemned as a false prophet and hacked to pieces. So the prophet who gets it wrong once is seen no more.

Prophecy is a gift of God.[16] That is why abusing it should be treated as a punishable deceit. Among the Scythians, whenever their soothsayers got it wrong they were shackled hand and foot and laid in ox-carts full of bracken where they were burned.[17] Those who treat subjects under the guidance of human limitations can be excused if they have done their best; but those who come and cheat us with assurances of powers beyond the natural order and then fail to do what they promise, should they not be punished for it and for the foolhardiness of their deceit?

These peoples have their wars against others further inland beyond their mountains; they go forth naked, with

16. Cf. Cicero, *De divinatione*, I, i.1; I Peter 1:2; I Corinthians 12:20; 13.2.

17. Herodotus, *History*, IV, lxix.

no other arms but their bows and their wooden swords sharpened to a point like the blades of our pig-stickers. Their steadfastness in battle is astonishing and always ends in killing and bloodshed: they do not even know the meaning of fear or flight. Each man brings back the head of the enemy he has slain and sets it as a trophy over the door of his dwelling. For a long period they treat captives well and provide them with all the comforts which they can devise; afterwards the master of each captive summons a great assembly of his acquaintances; he ties a rope to one of the arms of his prisoner and holds him by it, standing a few feet away for fear of being caught in the blows, and allows his dearest friend to hold the prisoner the same way by the other arm: then, before the whole assembly, they both hack at him with their swords and kill him. This done, they roast him and make a common meal of him, sending chunks of his flesh to absent friends. This is not as some think done for food – as the Scythians used to do in antiquity – but to symbolize ultimate revenge. As a proof of this, when they noted that the Portuguese who were allied to their enemies practised a different kind of execution on them when taken prisoner – which was to bury them up to the waist, to shoot showers of arrows at their exposed parts and then to hang them – they thought that these men from the Other World, who had scattered a knowledge of many a vice throughout their neighbour- 15 hood and who were greater masters than they were of every kind of revenge, which must be more severe than their own; so they began to abandon their ancient method and adopted that one. It does not sadden me that we should note the horrible barbarity in a practice such as theirs: what does sadden me is that, while judging correctly of their wrong-doings we should be so blind to our own. I think there is more barbarity in eating a man alive than in eating him dead; more barbarity in lacerating by rack and torture a body still fully able to feel things, in roasting him little by little and having him bruised and bitten by pigs and dogs (as we have not only read about but seen in recent memory, not among enemies in antiquity but among our fellow-citizens and neighbours – and, what is worse, in the name of duty and religion) than in roasting him and eating him after his death.

Chrysippus and Zeno, the leaders of the Stoic school, certainly thought that there was nothing wrong in using our carcasses for whatever purpose we needed, even for food – as our own forebears did when, beleaguered by Caesar in the town of Alesia, they decided to relieve the hunger of the besieged with the flesh of old men, women and others who were no use in battle:

> *Vascones, fama est, alimentis talibus usi*
> *Produxere animas.*

[By the eating of such food it is notorious that the Gascons prolonged their lives.][18]

And our medical men do not flinch from using corpses in many ways, both internally and externally, to cure us.[19] Yet no opinion has ever been so unruly as to justify treachery, disloyalty, tyranny and cruelty, which are everyday vices in us. So we can indeed call those folk barbarians by the rules of reason but not in comparison with ourselves, who surpass them in every kind of barbarism. Their warfare is entirely noble and magnanimous; it has as much justification and beauty as that human malady allows: among them it has no other foundation than a zealous concern for courage. They are not striving to conquer new lands, since without toil or travail they still enjoy that bounteous Nature who furnishes them abundantly with all they need, so that they have no concern to push back their frontiers. They are still in that blessed state of desiring nothing beyond what is ordained by their natural necessities: for them anything further is merely superfluous. The generic term which they use for men of the same age is 'brother'; younger men they call 'sons'. As

18. Sextus Empiricus, *Hypotyposes*, III, xxiv; Caesar, *Gallic Wars*, VII, lvii–lviii; Juvenal, *Satires*, XV, 93–4.

19. Mummies were imported for use in medicines. (Othello's handkerchief was steeped in 'juice of mummy'.)

for the old men, they are the 'fathers' of everyone else; they bequeath all their goods, indivisibly, to all these heirs in common, there being no other entitlement than that with which Nature purely and simply endows all her creatures by bringing them into this world. If the neighbouring peoples come over the mountains to attack them and happen to defeat them, the victors' booty consists in fame and in the privilege of mastery in virtue and valour: they have no other interest in the goods of the vanquished and so return home to their own land, which lacks no necessity; nor do they lack that great accomplishment of knowing how to enjoy their mode-of-being in happiness and to be content with it. These people do the same in their turn: they require no other ransom from their prisoners-of-war than that they should admit and acknowledge their defeat – yet there is not one prisoner in a hundred years who does not prefer to die rather than to derogate from the greatness of an invincible mind by look or by word; you cannot find one who does not prefer to be killed and eaten than merely to ask to be spared. In order to make their prisoners love life more they treat them generously in every way,[20] but occupy their thoughts with the menaces of the death awaiting all of them, of the

20. '80: generously in every way, *and furnish them with all the comforts they can devise* but . . .

tortures they will have to undergo and of the preparations being made for it, of limbs to be lopped off and of the feast they will provide. All that has only one purpose: to wrench some weak or unworthy word from their lips or to make them wish to escape, so as to enjoy the privilege of having frightened them and forced their constancy.[21]

Indeed, if you take it the right way, true victory[22] consists in that alone:

victoria nulla est
Quam quæ confessos animo quoque subjugat hostes.

[There is no victory unless you subjugate the minds
of the enemy and make them admit defeat.][23]

In former times those warlike fighters the Hungarians never pressed their advantage beyond making their enemy throw himself on their mercy. Once having wrenched this admission from him, they let him go without injury or ransom, except at most for an undertaking never again to bear arms against them.[24]

Quite enough of the advantages we do gain over our

---

21. '80: their *virtue and their* constancy . . .
22. '80: true *and solid* victory . . .
23. Claudian, *De sexto consulatu Honorii*, 248–9.
24. Nicolas Chalcocondylas (tr. Blaise de Vigenère), *De la décadence de l'empire grec*, V, ix.

enemies are mainly borrowed ones not truly our own. To have stronger arms and legs is the property of a porter not of Valour; agility is a dead and physical quality, for it is chance which causes your opponent to stumble and which makes the sun dazzle him; to be good at fencing is a matter of skill and knowledge which may light on a coward or a worthless individual. A man's worth and reputation lie in the mind and in the will: his true honour is found there. Bravery does not consist in firm arms and legs but in firm minds and souls: it is not a matter of what our horse or our weapons are worth but of what we are. The man who is struck down but whose mind remains steadfast, 'si succiderit, de genu pugnat' [if his legs give way, then on his knees doth he fight];[25] the man who relaxes none of his mental assurance when threatened with imminent death and who faces his enemy with inflexible scorn as he gives up the ghost is beaten by Fortune not by us: he is slain but not vanquished.[26] Sometimes it is the bravest who may prove most unlucky. So there are triumphant defeats rivalling victories; Salamis, Plataea, Mycale and Sicily are the fairest sister-victories which the Sun has ever seen, yet they would never dare to compare their

25. Seneca, *De constantia*, II.
26. '80: by us: *he is vanquished in practice but not by reason; it is his bad luck which we may indict not his cowardice.* Sometimes . . .

combined glory with the glorious defeat of King Leonidas and his men at the defile of Thermopylae.[27] Who has ever run into battle with a greater desire and ambition for victory than did Captain Ischolas when he was defeated? Has any man ever assured his safety more cleverly or carefully than he assured his destruction?[28] His task was to defend against the Arcadians a certain pass in the Peloponnesus. He realized that he could not achieve this because of the nature of the site and of the odds against him, concluding that every man who faced the enemy must of necessity die in the battlefield; on the other hand he judged it unworthy of his own courage, of his greatness of soul and of the name of Sparta to fail in his duty; so he chose the middle path between these two extremes and acted thus: he saved the youngest and fittest soldiers of his unit to serve for the defence of their country and sent them back there. He then determined to defend that pass with men whose loss would matter less and who would, by their death, make the enemy purchase their breakthrough as dearly as possible. And so it turned out. After butchering the Arcadians who beset them on every side, they were all put to the sword. Was ever a trophy raised to a

27. Cf. Cicero, *Tusc. disput.*, I, xli, 100 for the glory of Leonidas' death in the defile of Thermopylae.
28. Diodorus Siculus, XV, xii.

victor which was not better due to those who were vanquished? True victory lies in your role in the conflict, not in coming through safely: it consists in the honour of battling bravely not battling through.

To return to my tale, those prisoners, far from yielding despite all that was done to them during the two or three months of their captivity, maintain on the contrary a joyful countenance: they urge their captors to hurry up and put them to the test; they defy them, insult them and reproach them for cowardice and for all the battles they have lost against their country. I have a song made by one such prisoner which contains the following: Let them all dare to come and gather to feast on him, for with him they will feast on their own fathers and ancestors who have served as food and sustenance for his body. 'These sinews,' he said, 'this flesh and these veins – poor fools that you are – are your very own; you do not realize that they still contain the very substance of the limbs of your forebears: savour them well, for you will find that they taste of your very own flesh!' There is nothing 'barbarous' in the contriving of that topic. Those who tell how they die and who describe the act of execution show the prisoners spitting at their killers and pulling faces at them. Indeed, until their latest breath, they never stop braving them and defying them with word and look. It is no lie to say that these men are indeed savages – by our standards;

for either they must be or we must be: there is an amazing gulf between their souls and ours.[29]

The husbands have several wives: the higher their reputation for valour the more of them they have. One beautiful characteristic of their marriages is worth noting: just as our wives are zealous in thwarting our love and tenderness for other women, theirs are equally zealous in obtaining them for them. Being more concerned for their husband's reputation than for anything else, they take care and trouble to have as many fellow-wives as possible, since that is a testimony to their husband's valour.

– Our wives will scream that that is a marvel, but it is not: it is a virtue proper to matrimony, but at an earlier stage. In the Bible Leah, Rachel, Sarah and the wives of Jacob all made their fair handmaidens available to their husbands; Livia, to her own detriment, connived at the lusts of Augustus, and Stratonice the consort of King Deiotarus not only provided her husband with a very beautiful chambermaid who served her but carefully brought up their children and lent a hand in enabling them to succeed to her husband's rank.[30]

---

29. '80: their *constancy* and ours . . .

30. Standard examples: cf. Tiraquellus, *De legibus connubialibus*, XIII, 35, for all these un-jealous wives. (But Leah and Sarah were, in fact, Jacob's wives.)

– Lest anyone should think that they do all this out of a simple slavish subjection to convention or because of the impact of the authority of their ancient customs without any reasoning or judgement on their part, having minds so dulled that they could never decide to do anything else, I should cite a few examples of what they are capable of.

Apart from that war-song which I have just given an account of, I have another of their songs, a love-song, which begins like this:

> O Adder, stay: stay O Adder! From your colours
> let my sister take the pattern for a girdle
> she will make for me to offer to my love;
> So may your beauty and your speckled hues be for
> ever honoured above all other snakes.

This opening couplet serves as the song's refrain. Now I know enough about poetry to make the following judgement: not only is there nothing 'barbarous' in this conceit but it is thoroughly anacreontic.[31] Their language incidentally is a pleasant one with an agreeable sound and has terminations[32] rather like Greek.

31. Anacreon was the great love-poet of Teos (*fl.* 540 BC).
32. '80: their language *is the pleasantest language in the world; its* sound *is agreeable to the ear* and has terminations . . .

Three such natives, unaware of what price in peace and happiness they would have to pay to buy a knowledge of our corruptions, and unaware that such commerce would lead to their downfall – which I suspect to be already far advanced – pitifully allowing themselves to be cheated by their desire for novelty and leaving the gentleness of their regions to come and see ours, were at Rouen at the same time as King Charles IX.[33] The King had a long interview with them: they were shown our manners, our ceremonial and the layout of a fair city. Then someone asked them what they thought of all this and wanted to know what they had been most amazed by. They made three points; I am very annoyed with myself for forgetting the third, but I still remember two of them. In the first place they said (probably referring to the Swiss Guard) that they found it very odd that all those full-grown bearded men, strong and bearing arms in the King's entourage, should consent to obey a boy rather than choosing one of themselves as a Commander; secondly – since they have an idiom in their language which calls all men 'halves' of one another – that they had noticed that there were among us men fully bloated with all sorts of comforts while their halves were begging at their doors, emaciated with poverty and hunger: they found it odd that those destitute halves should put

33. In 1562, when Rouen was retaken by Royalist forces.

up with such injustice and did not take the others by the throat or set fire to their houses.

I had a very long talk with one of them (but I used a stupid interpreter who was so bad at grasping my meaning and at understanding my ideas that I got little joy from it). When I asked the man (who was a commander among them, our sailors calling him a king) what advantage he got from his high rank, he told me that it was to lead his troops into battle; asked how many men followed him, he pointed to an open space to signify as many as it would hold – about four or five thousand men; questioned whether his authority lapsed when the war was over, he replied that he retained the privilege of having paths cut for him through the thickets in their forests, so that he could easily walk through them when he visited villages under his sway.

Not at all bad, that. – Ah! But they wear no breeches . . .

On Smells

[*An early compilation which progressively becomes more personal: the topic itself may have been suggested by a commonplace of the* Querelle des femmes *(the centuries-long series of works for and against women and marriage)*.]

Of some such as Alexander the Great it is said that their sweat smelt nice (because of some rare complexion outside the natural Order, the cause of which was sought by Plutarch and others).[1] But the normal fashioning of our bodies works contrary to that: the best characteristic we can hope for is to smell of nothing. The sweetness of the purest breath consists in nothing more excellent than to be without any offensive smell, as the breath of healthy children. That is why Plautus says, '*Mulier tum bene olet, ubi nihil olet*', 'A woman smells nice when she smells of nothing', just as we say that the best perfume for her actions is for her to be quiet and discreet.[2] And when

---

1. Plutarch (tr. Amyot), *Propos de table*, 366C.
2. Plautus, *Mustellaria*, I, iii, 117; cf. Tiraquellus, *De legibus connubialibus*, III, §§9–10.

people give off nice odours which are not their own we may rightly suspect them, and conclude that they use them to smother some natural stench. That is what gives rise to those adages of the ancient poets which claim that the man who smells nice in fact stinks:

> *Rides nos Coracine, nil olentes.*
> *Malo quam bene olere, nil olere.*

[You laugh at us, Coracinus, because we emit no smell:
I would rather smell of nothing than smell sweetly.]

And again,

> *Posthume, non bene olet, qui bene semper olet.*

[A man who always smells nice, Posthumus, actually stinks.][3]

However I am myself very fond of living amongst good smells and I immeasurably loathe bad ones, which I sense at a greater distance than anyone else:

> *Namque sagacius unus odoror,*
> *Polypus, an gravis hirsutis cubet hircus in alis,*
> *Quam canis acer ubi lateat sus.*

3. Martial, VI, lv, 4–5; II, xii, 4 (both in Tiraquellus, loc. cit.).

[I have a nose with more flair, Polypus, for sensing
the goaty smell of hairy armpits than any hound on the
track of a stinking boar.][4]

The simpler, more natural smells seem to me to be the
most agreeable. A concern for smells is chiefly a matter
for the ladies. In deepest Barbary the Scythian women
powder themselves after washing and smother their whole
face and body with a certain sweet-smelling unguent,
native to their soil; when they take off this cosmetic they
find themselves smooth and nice-smelling for an approach
to their menfolk.

Whatever the smell, it is wonderful how it clings to me
and how my skin is simply made to drink it in. The
person who complained that Nature left Man with no
means of bringing smells to his nose was in error: smells
do it by themselves. But, in my particular case the job is
done for me by my thick moustache: if I bring my glove
or my handkerchief anywhere near it, the smell will linger
there all day. It gives away where I have just come from.
Those close smacking kisses of my youth, gluey and
greedy, would stick to it and remain there for hours
afterwards. Yet I find myself little subject to those mass
illnesses which are caught by social intercourse and spring

4. Horace, *Epodes*, XII, 4–7.

from infected air; and I have been spared those of my own time, of which there have been several kinds in our towns and among our troops. We read that although Socrates never left Athens during several recurrences of the plague which so often racked that city, he alone suffered no harm.[5]

It seems to me that doctors could make better use of smells than they do, for I have frequently noticed that, depending on which they are, they variously affect me and work upon my animal spirits;[6] which convinces me of the truth of what is said about the invention of odours and incense in our Churches (a practice so ancient and so widespread among all nations and religions): that it was aimed at making us rejoice, exciting us and purifying us so as to render us more capable of contemplation.

In order to judge it I wish I had been invited to experience the culinary art of those chefs who know how to season wafting odours with the savour of various foods, as was particularly remarked in our time in the case of the King of Tunis who landed at Naples for face to face talks with the Emperor Charles. His meats were stuffed with sweet-smelling ingredients, so luxuriously that a peacock

5. Diogenes Laertius, *Life of Socrates*.
6. 'Animal spirits' are the elements in man, separable from the body, which it animates.

and two pheasants cost a hundred ducats to prepare in their manner. And when those birds were cut up they filled not merely the hall but all the rooms of his palace and even the neighbouring houses with a delicious mist which was slow to evaporate.

When choosing where to stay, my principal concern is to avoid air which is oppressive and stinking. My liking for those fair cities Venice and Paris is affected by the pungent smell of the marshes of one and the mud of the other.[7]

7. In Venice the stench of the canals produced 'bad air' (*malaria*). As for Paris, Joachim Du Bellay emphasizes how its mud struck him on his return from Rome (*Regrets*, 138).

On the Art of Conversation

[*French children know that Pascal referred to Montaigne as 'the incomparable author of "The art of conversation"'. That has given this chapter a special place in French culture. It is further valued for the light it throws on to Montaigne's character. The conversation in this chapter turns to Tacitus and shows us how Montaigne had conversations with himself about the books he was reading.*]

It is a custom of our justice to punish some as a warning to others. For to punish them for *having done* wrong would, as Plato says, be stupid: what is done cannot be undone. The intention is to stop them from repeating the same mistake or to make others avoid their error.[1] We do not improve the man we hang: we improve others by him. I do the same. My defects are becoming natural and incorrigible, but as fine gentlemen serve the public as models to follow I may serve a turn as a model to avoid:

1. Plato, *Laws*, XI, 934 A–B.

Nonne vides Albi ut male vivat filius, utque
Barrus inops? magnum documentum, ne patriam rem
Perdere quis velit

[You can see, can't you, how wretchedly Albus'
son is living and how poor Barrus is? An excellent lesson
in not squandering your inheritance.][2]

The act of publishing and indicting my imperfections
may teach someone how to fear them. (The talents which
I most esteem in myself derive more honour from[3] indicting me than praising me.) That is why I so often return to
it and linger over it. Yet, when all has been said, you
never talk about yourself without loss: condemn yourself
and you are always believed: praise yourself and you never
are.

There may be others of my complexion who learn
better by counter-example than by example, by eschewing
not pursuing. That was the sort of instruction which the
Elder Cato was thinking of when he said that the wise
have more to learn from the fools than the fools from the
wise;[4] as also that lyre-player in antiquity who, Pausanias

2. Horace, *Satires*, I, iv, 109–11.
3. '88: more *advantage* from . . .
4. Erasmus, *Apophthegmata*, V, *Cato Senior*, XXXIX.

says, used to require his students to go and listen to some performer who lived across the street so that they would learn to loathe discords and faulty rhythms.[5] My horror of cruelty thrusts me deeper into clemency than any example of clemency ever could draw me. A good equerry does not make me sit up straight in the saddle as much as the sight of a lawyer or a Venetian out riding, and a bad use of language corrects my own better than a good one. Every day I am warned and counselled by the stupid deportment of someone. What hits you affects you and wakes you up more than what pleases you. We can only improve ourselves in times such as these by walking backwards, by discord not by harmony, by being different not by being like. Having myself learned little from good examples I use the bad ones, the text of which is routine. I strove to be as agreeable as others were seen to be boring; as firm as others were flabby; as gentle as others were sharp. But I was setting myself unattainable standards.[6]

To my taste the most fruitful and most natural exercise of our minds is conversation. I find the practice of it the most delightful activity in our lives. That is why, if I were

---

5. Anecdote not traced. Perhaps a confusion with the practice of the ancient musician Timotheus of Miletus. Cf. Quintilian, II, iii, 3.

6. '88: routine: *the routine sight of thieving and perfidiousness has guided and restrained my morals.* To my taste . . .

now obliged to make the choice, I think I would rather lose my sight than my powers of speech or hearing. In their academies the Athenians, and even more the Romans, maintained this exercise in great honour. In our own times the Italians retain some vestiges of it – greatly to their benefit, as can be seen from a comparison of their intelligence and ours. Studying books has a languid feeble motion, whereas conversation provides teaching and exercise all at once. If I am sparring with a strong and solid opponent he will attack me on the flanks, stick his lance in me right and left; his ideas send mine soaring. Rivalry, competitiveness and glory will drive me and raise me above my own level. In conversation the most painful quality is perfect harmony.

Just as our mind is strengthened by contact with vigorous and well-ordered minds, so too it is impossible to overstate how much it loses and deteriorates by the continuous commerce and contact we have with mean and ailing ones. No infection is as contagious as that is. I know by experience what that costs by the ell. I love arguing and discussing, but with only a few men and for my own sake: for to serve as a spectacle to the great and indulge in a parade of your wits and your verbiage is, I consider, an unbecoming trade for an honourable gentleman.

Stupidity is a bad quality: but to be unable to put up   35

with it, to be vexed and ground down by it (as happens to me) is another, hardly worse in its unmannerliness than stupidity. And that is what at present I wish to condemn in myself.

I embark upon discussion and argument with great ease and liberty. Since opinions do not find in me a ready soil to thrust and spread their roots into, no premise shocks me, no belief hurts me, no matter how opposite to my own they may be. There is no idea so frivolous or odd which does not appear to me to be fittingly produced by the mind of man. Those of us who deprive our judgement of the right to pass sentence look gently on strange opinions; we may not lend them our approbation but we do readily lend them our ears. When one scale in the balance is quite empty I will let the other be swayed by an old woman's dreams: so it seems pardonable if I choose the odd number rather than the even, or Thursday rather than Friday; if I prefer to be twelfth or fourteenth at table rather than thirteenth; if I prefer on my travels to see a hare skirting my path rather than crossing it, and offer my left foot to be booted before the right. All such lunacies (which are believed among us) at least deserve to be heard. For me they only outweigh an empty scale, but outweigh it they do. Similarly the weight of popular and unfounded opinions has a natural existence which is more

than nothing. A man who will not go that far perhaps

avoids the vice of superstition by falling into the vice of stubbornness.

So contradictory judgements neither offend me nor irritate me: they merely wake me up and provide me with exercise. We avoid being corrected: we ought to come forward and accept it, especially when it comes from conversation not a lecture. Whenever we meet opposition, we do not look to see if it is just but how we can get out of it, rightly or wrongly. Instead of welcoming arms we stretch out our claws. I can put up with being roughly handled by my friends: 'You are an idiot! You are raving!' Among gentlemen I like people to express themselves heartily, their words following wherever their thoughts lead. We ought to toughen and fortify our ears against being seduced by the sound of polite words. I like a strong, intimate, manly fellowship, the kind of friendship which rejoices in sharp vigorous exchanges just as love rejoices in bites and scratches which draw blood. It is not strong enough nor magnanimous enough if it is not argumentative, if all is politeness and art; if it is afraid of clashes and walks hobbled. '*Neque enim disputari sine reprehensione potest.*' [It is impossible to debate without refuting.][7]

When I am contradicted it arouses my attention not my

7. Cicero, *De finibus*, I, viii, 28 (Torquatus defending Epicurus' style of conversation).

wrath. I move towards the man who contradicts me: he is instructing me. The cause of truth ought to be common to us both. – What will his answer be? The passion of anger has already wounded his judgement. Turbulence has seized it before reason can. – It would be a useful idea if we had to wager on the deciding of our quarrels, useful if there were a material sign of our defeats so that we could keep tally on them and my manservant say: 'Last year your ignorance and stubbornness cost you one hundred crowns on twenty occasions.'

I welcome truth, I fondle it, in whosesoever hand I find it; I surrender to it cheerfully, welcoming it with my vanquished arms as soon as I see it approaching from afar. And provided that they do not set about it with too imperious and schoolmasterish a frown I will put my shoulder to the wheel to help along the criticisms that people make of my writings: I have often made changes more for reasons of politeness than to effect reasonable corrections, preferring to please and encourage people's freedom to criticize me by my readiness to give way – yes, even when it cost me something. Yet it is difficult to attract men to do that in our days. They have no stomach for correcting because they have no stomach for suffering correction, always dissembling when talking in each other's presence.

I take such great pleasure in being judged and known

that it is virtually indifferent to me which of the two forms it takes. My thought so often contradicts and condemns itself that it is all one to me if someone else does so, seeing that I give to his refutation only such authority as I please. But I fall out with anyone who is too high-handed, like one man I know who laments the fact that he gave you advice if you do not accept it and takes it as an insult if you shy at following it.

Socrates always laughingly welcomed contradictions made to his arguments. It could be said that since his arguments were the stronger the advantage would always fall to him and that he welcomed them as matter for fresh triumphs: but we, on the contrary, find that there is nothing which makes us more susceptible than convictions about our own surpassing excellence, our contempt for our adversary, and about its being reasonable for the weaker to be willing to accept refutations which set him back on his feet and redress him.

I do truly seek to frequent those who manhandle me rather than those who are afraid of me. It is a bland and harmful pleasure to have to deal with people who admire us and defer to us. Antisthenes commanded his sons never to give thanks or show gratitude to anyone who praised them.[8] I feel far prouder of the victory I win over myself

8. Plutarch (tr. Amyot), *De la mauvaise honte*, 81 B.

when I make myself give way beneath my adversary's powers of reason in the heat of battle than I ever feel gratified by the victory I win over him through his weakness. In short I admit and acknowledge any attacks, no matter how feeble, if they are made directly, but I am all too impatient of attacks which are not made in due form. I care little about what we are discussing; all opinions are the same to me and it is all but indifferent to me which proposition emerges victorious. I can go on peacefully arguing all day if the debate is conducted with due order. It is not so much forceful and subtle argument that I want as order – the kind of order which can be found every day in disputes among shepherds and shop-assistants yet never among us. If they go astray it is in lack of courtesy. So do we. But their stormy intolerance does not make them stray far from their theme: their arguments keep on course. They interrupt each other. They jostle, but at least get the gist. To answer the point is, in my judgement, to answer very well. But when the discussion becomes turbulent and lacks order, I quit the subject-matter and cling irritably and injudiciously to the form, dashing into a style of debate which is stubborn, ill-willed and imperious, one which I have to blush for later.

It is impossible to argue in good faith with a fool. Not only my judgement is corrupted at the hands of so violent a master, so is my sense of right and wrong. Our quarrels ought to be outlawed and punished as are other verbal crimes. Since they are always ruled and governed by anger, what vices do they not awaken and pile up on each other? First we feel enmity for the arguments and then for the men. In debating we are taught merely how to refute arguments; the result of each side's refuting the other is that the fruit of our debates is the destruction and annihilation of the truth.[9] That is why Plato in his *Republic* prohibits that exercise to ill-endowed minds not suited to it.[10]

You are in quest of what *is*.[11] Why on earth do you set out to walk that road with a man who has neither pace nor style? We do no wrong to the subject-matter if we depart from it in order to examine the way to treat it — I do not mean a scholastic, donnish way, I mean a natural way, based on a healthy intellect. But what happens in the end? One goes east and the other west; they lose the fundamental point in the confusion of a mass of incidentals. After a tempestuous hour they no longer know what they are looking for. One man is beside the bull's eye, the other too

9. Renaissance rhetoric and dialectic in school and university did indeed often encourage *pro et contra* debates rather than a search for truth.

10. Plato, *Republic*, 539 A–C.

11. '88: of *the truth*: why . . .

high, the other too low. One fastens on a word or a comparison; another no longer sees his opponent's arguments, being too caught up in his own train of thought: he is thinking of pursuing his own argument not yours. Another, realizing he is too weak in the loins, is afraid of everything, denies everything and, from the outset, muddles and confuses the argument, or else, at the climax of the debate he falls into a rebellious total silence, affecting, out of morose ignorance, a haughty disdain or an absurdly modest desire to avoid contention. Yet[12] another does not care how much he drops his own guard provided that he can hit you. Another counts every word and believes they are as weighty as reasons. This man merely exploits the superior power of his voice and lungs. And then there is the man who sums up against himself; and the other who deafens you with useless introductions and digressions. Another is armed with pure insults and picks a groundless 'German quarrel' so as to free himself from the company and conversation of a mind which presses hard on his own.

Lastly, there is the man who cannot see reason but holds you under siege within a hedge of dialectical conclusions and logical formulae. Who can avoid beginning to distrust our professional skills and doubt whether we can extract from them any solid profit of practical use in life

12. '88: muddles *and ruffles the debate*. Yet another . . .

when he reflects on the use we put them to? '*Nihil sanantibus litteris.*' [such erudition as has no power to heal.][13] Has anyone ever acquired intelligence through logic? Where are her beautiful promises? '*Nec ad melius vivendum nec ad commodius disserendum.*' [She teaches neither how to live a better life nor how to argue properly.] Is there more of a hotchpotch in the cackle of fishwives than in the public disputations of men who profess logic? I would prefer a son of mine to learn to talk in the tavern rather than in our university yap-shops.

Take an arts don; converse with him. Why is he incapable of making us feel the excellence of his 'arts' and of throwing the women, and us ignoramuses, into ecstasies of admiration at the solidity of his arguments and the beauty of his ordered rhetoric! Why cannot he overmaster us and sway us at his will? Why does a man with his superior mastery of matter and style intermingle his sharp thrusts with insults, indiscriminate arguments and rage? Let him remove his academic hood, his gown and his Latin; let him stop battering our ears with raw chunks of pure Aristotle; why, you would take him for one of us – or worse. The involved linguistic convolutions with which they confound us remind me of conjuring tricks: their

13. Seneca, *Epist. moral.*, LIX, 15; then, Cicero, *De finibus*, I, xix, 63, criticizing Epicurean logic.

sleight-of-hand has compelling force over our senses but it in no wise shakes our convictions. Apart from such jugglery they achieve nothing but what is base and ordinary. They may be more learned but they are no less absurd.

I like and honour erudition as much as those who have it. When used properly it is the most noble and powerful acquisition of Man. But in the kind of men (and their number is infinite) who make it the base and foundation of their worth and achievement, who quit their understanding for their memory, '*sub aliena umbra latentes*' [hiding behind other men's shadows],[14] and can do nothing except by book, I loathe (dare I say it?) a little more than I loathe stupidity.

In my part of the country and during my own lifetime school-learning has brought amendment of purse but rarely amendment of soul. If the souls it meets are already obtuse, as a raw and undigested mass it clogs and suffocates them; if they are unfettered, it tends to purge them, strip them of impurities and volatilize them into vacuity. Erudition is a thing the quality of which is neither good nor bad, almost: it is a most useful adjunct to a well-endowed soul: to any other it is baleful and harmful; or rather, it is a thing which, in use, has great value,[15] but it

---

14. Seneca, *Epist. moral.*, XXXIII, 7.

15. '88: great *nobility and* value . . .

will not allow itself to be acquired at a base price: in one hand it is a royal sceptre, in another, a fool's bauble.

But to get on: what greater victory do you want than to teach your enemy that he cannot stand up to you? Get the better of him by your argument and the winner is the truth; do so by your order and style, then you are the winner!

I am persuaded that, in both Plato and Xenophon, Socrates debates more for the debater's than for debating's sake; more to teach Euthydemus and Protagoras their own absurdity than the absurdity of their sophists' art. He seizes hold of the first subject which comes to hand, as a man who has a more useful aim than to throw light on his subject as such: namely, to enlighten the minds which he accepts to train and to exercise. The game which we hunt is the fun of the chase: we are inexcusable if we pursue it badly or foolishly: it is quite another thing if we fail to make a kill. For we are born to go in quest of truth: to take possession of it is the property of a greater Power.[16] Truth is not (as Democritus said) hidden in the bottom of an abyss: it is, rather, raised infinitely high within the knowledge of God.[17]

---

16. The theme of III, 13, 'On experience'.

17. For Democritus, cf. Cicero, *Academica*, I, xii, 44: a celebrated saying of Democritus, cited similarly to Montaigne by the Christian

45

This world is but a school of inquiry. The question is not who will spear the ring but who will make the best charges at it. The man who says what is true can act as foolishly as the one who says what is untrue: we are talking about the way you say it not what you say. My humour is to consider the form as much as the substance, and the barrister as much as his case, as Alcibiades told us to.[18] Every day I spend time reading my authors, not caring about their learning, looking not for their subject-matter but how they handle it; just as I go in pursuit of discussions with a celebrated mind not to be taught by it but to get to know it.

Any man may speak truly: few men can speak ordinately, wisely, adequately. And so errors which proceed from ignorance do not offend me: absurdity does. I have often broken off discussing a bargain, even one advantageous to me, because of the silly claims of those I was bargaining with. For their mistakes I do not lose my temper above once a year with any of those who are subject to my authority, but when the point is the stupidity

---

theologian Lactantius, *Institutiones divinarum* III, 28, a reference given in the adage *Veritas in profundo* (*Appendix Erasmi*, in *Adagia id est Proverbiorum collectio absolutissima*, Frankfurt, 1656, p. 453).

18. Perhaps an echo of the similar remark attributed to him in Henry Estienne's *Apophthegmata*, 1588, pp. 110–11.

of their assertions or the obstinacy of their asinine excuses and their daft defences, then we are daily at each other's throats. They understand neither why nor what they are told: they answer accordingly. It is enough to make you despair. It is only when my head bangs against another head that I feel a big bump: I can come to terms with the failings of my servants better than with their thoughtlessness, insolence and downright silliness. Let them do less, provided that they can do something! You live in hope of making their wills warm to their work: but there is nothing to get from a blockhead, nothing to hope for.

Yes, but what if I myself am taking things for other than they are? That may well be: that explains first of all why I condemn my inability to put up with it, holding it to be equally a defect in those who are right and those who are wrong, since there is always an element of tyrannical bad temper in being unable to tolerate characters different from your own. Secondly, there is in truth no greater silliness, none more enduring, than to be provoked and enraged by the silliness of this world – and there is none more bizarre. For it makes you principally irritated with yourself: that philosopher of old would never have lacked occasion for his tears if he had concentrated on himself.[19] One of the Seven Sages, Myson, was of the

19. Heraclitus, the Sage who wept at the folly of the world; normally   47

same humour as Timon and Democritus: when asked what he was laughing at all by himself, he replied, 'At the fact that I am laughing all by myself.'

How many statements and replies do I make every day which are silly by my norms – so even more frequently, to be sure, by the standards of others![20] If I bite my lips for them, what must the others be doing! To sum up, we have to live among the living and let the stream flow under the bridge without worrying about it or, at very least, without making ourselves ill over it. Indeed, why can we encounter a man with a twisted deformed body without getting irritated, yet are unable to tolerate a deranged mind without flying into a rage?[21] Such harshness is vitiated and derives from the critic rather than the fault. Let us always have Plato's saying on our lips: 'If I find ill in something may it not be because I myself am ill? Am I not the one at fault? May my own criticism not be turned against me?' A wise and inspired refrain which chastises the most common and universal error of mankind. It is not merely the reproaches which we make to each other

---

coupled with Democritus, who laughed at it. Followed by the most famous saying of Myson (Erasmus, *Apophthegmata*, VII, *Myson*, I).

20. Literally silly '*selon moy*' (that is, by my own terms of reference), even sillier 'according to others' (by their terms of reference).

21. Plutarch (tr. Amyot), *Comment on pourra recevoir utilité de ses ennemis*, 110 E–F (and for Plato's saying about to be quoted).

which can be regularly turned against us but also our
reasons and our arguments in matters of controversy: we
run ourselves through with our own swords. As it was
ingeniously and aptly put by the man who first said it:
'*Stercus cuique suum bene olet.*' [Everyone's shit smells
good to himself.][22]

Our eyes see nothing behind us.[23] A hundred times a
day when we go mocking our neighbour we are really
mocking ourselves; we abominate in others those faults
which are most manifestly our own, and, with a miraculous
lack of shame and perspicacity, are astonished by them.
Only yesterday I was able to watch an intelligent nobleman
making jokes, as good as they were pertinent, about
the silly way in which another nobleman went bashing

22. Erasmus, *Adages*, III, IV, II. Erasmus links the saying to
Aristotle's *Nicomachaean Ethics*, and to the complementary adage,
Suum cuique pulchrum (one's own is beautiful to oneself) (I, II, XV),
further linked with Plato, Aristotle and Horace as a condemnation of
philautia (self-love).

23. Another authoritative condemnation of self-love, in Aesop's
Beggar's Wallet: we put our neighbours' faults in the front pocket
where we can see them, our own in the back one where we cannot.
(Cf. Rabelais, TLF, *Tiers Livre*, TLF, XV, note 108, citing Erasmus'
Adages and Raymond Sebond.)

'88: olet. *To sum up, we must live among the living and let each man
follow his fashion without our worrying or without making ourselves ill
about it.*

49

everyone's ear about his family-tree and his family alliances, more than half of which were false, that kind of man being most inclined to launch out on such stupid subjects when his escutcheon is more dubious and least certain: yet he too, if he had stood back and looked at himself, would have discovered that he was hardly less extravagant in broadcasting and less boring in stressing the claims to precedence of his wife's family. What a dangerous arrogance with which a wife is seen to be armed at the hands of her very husband! If they understood Latin we ought to say to such people:

Age! si hæc non insanit satis sua sponte, instiga!

[That's the way! If she is not mad enough herself, egg her on!][24]

I do not mean that nobody should make indictments unless he is spotless; if that were so, no one would make them. What I mean is that when our judgement brings a charge against another man over a matter then in question, it must not exempt us from an internal judicial inquiry. It is a work of charity for a man who is unable to weed out a defect in himself to try, nevertheless, to weed it out in another in whom the seedling may be less malignant and stubborn. And it never seems to me to be an appropriate

24. Terence, *Andria*, IV, ii, 9.

answer to anyone who warns me of a fault in me to say that he has it too. What difference does that make? The warning remains true and useful. If we had sound nostrils our shit ought to stink all the more for its being our own. Socrates was convinced that if there was a man who, together with his son and a stranger, was found guilty of violence or injury, that man should begin with himself, first presenting himself to be sentenced by the judge and to beg for expiation at the hands of the executioner; next, he should present his son; then the stranger.[25] If that precept pitches it rather too high, at least he should be the first to be presented before his own conscience for punishment.

Our first judges are properly our senses, which perceive things only by their external accidents. No wonder then that in all the elements which contribute to our society there is such a constant and universal addition of surface appearances and ritual; with the result that the best and most effective part of our polities consists in that. We are always dealing with Man, whose nature is wondrously corporeal. Those who in recent years have wished to build up for us so contemplative and non-material an exercise of worship should not be astonished if there are those who think that it would have slipped and melted through their

25. Plato, *Gorgias*, 480 B–C.

fingers if it did not keep a hold among us as a mark, sign and means of division and of faction rather than for itself.[26]

It is the same in discussion: the gravity, academic robes and rank of the man who is speaking often lend credence to arguments which are vain and silly. Who could believe that so redoubtable a lord with so great a retinue does not have within him some more-than-ordinary talent, or that a man who is entrusted with so many missions and offices of state, a man so disdainful and so arrogant, is not cleverer than another man who bows to him from afar and whom nobody ever employs! Not only the words of such people but their very grimaces are watched and put to their account, each man striving to give them some fine solid significance. If they condescend to join in ordinary discussions and you show them anything but approval and reverence, they clobber you with the authority of their experience: they have heard this; they have seen that; they have done this: you are overwhelmed with cases. I would like to tell such men that the fruit of a surgeon's experience lies not in a recital of his operations nor in his reminding

26. Perhaps a reference to the members of the Reformed Church; it is often taken to be so. But is it not rather an allusion to ascetic movements within the Roman Catholic Church tending to devalue the body and elevate asceticism?

us that he has cured four patients of the plague and three of the gout, unless he knows how to extract from them material for forming his judgement and unless he knows how to convince us that he has been made wiser by the practice of his medical art.[27] So, in a consort of instruments, we do not hear the lute, the spinet and the flute but a global harmony, the fruit resulting from the combination of the entire group.

If they have been improved by their missions and their travels that should appear in the products of their understanding. It is not enough to relate our experiences: we must weigh them and group them; we must also have digested them and distilled them so as to draw out the reasons and conclusions they comport. There never were so many writing history! It is always good and profitable to listen to them, for they furnish us with ample instruction, fine and praiseworthy, from the storehouse of their memory: that is certainly of great value in helping us to live. But we are not looking for that at the moment: we are trying to find out whether the chroniclers and compilers are themselves worthy of praise.

27. Aristotle's contention in *Metaphysics*, I, 1, 980b–981a. Experience and experiments as such do not constitute the *art* of medicine: the *art* consists in a general inference drawn from it by a man's judgement.

I loathe all tyranny, both in speech and action. I like to brace myself against those trivial incidentals which cheat our judgement via our senses; and by keeping a watchful eye on men of extraordinary rank I have discovered that they are, for the most part, just like the rest of us:

> *Rarus enim ferme sensus communis in illa*
> *Fortuna.*

[Common sense is rare enough in that high station.][28]

Perhaps we esteem them and perceive them for less than they are, because they undertake to do more and so reveal themselves more. The porter must be stronger and tougher than his load. The man who has not had to use all his strength leaves you to guess whether he has any more in reserve, whether he has been assayed to the ultimate point: the man who succumbs under the weight betrays his limitations and the weakness of his shoulders. That is why, more than other people, so many of the learned can be seen to have inadequate souls. They could have been good farmers, good merchants, good craftsmen: their natural forces were tailored to such proportions. Knowledge is a very weighty thing: they sink beneath it. Their mental apparatus has not enough energy nor skill to display that

28. Juvenal, *Satires*, VIII, 73–4.

noble material and to apportion its strength, to exploit it and to make it help them. Knowledge can lodge only in a powerful nature: and that is very rare. Feeble minds, said Socrates, corrupt the dignity of philosophy when they handle it; she appears to be useless and defective when sheathed in a bad covering.[29]

That is how they grow rotten and besotted,

> *Humani qualis simulator simius oris,*
> *Quem puer arridens pretioso stamine serum*
> *Velavit, nudasque nates ac terga reliquit,*
> *Ludibrium mensis.*

[Like an ape, that imitator of the human face, which a boy dresses up, for a laugh, in precious silken robes, leaving the cheeks of its backside bare to amuse the guests at table.]

It is the same for those who rule over us and give orders, who hold the world in their hands: it is not enough for them to have an ordinary intelligence, to be able to achieve what we can. They are far beneath us if they are not way above us. Since they promise more, they owe more too; that is why keeping silent is not, in their case, merely a courteous and grave demeanour; it is also more often a profitable and gainful one. For when Megabysus

29. Perhaps a reference to Plato, *Republic*, VI, 495 C–D.

went to see Appelles in his studio, he long remained silent. But when he began to discourse on the works of art, he received this rude reprimand: 'While you kept silent you appeared to be a great Somebody because of your chains-of-office and your retinue, but now we have heard you talk the very apprentices in my workshop despise you.'[30] Those magnificent decorations, that grand estate would not tolerate ordinary plebeian ignorance in him, nor inappropriate comments on paintings: he should have maintained that outward presumed connoisseurship. For how many men in my time has a cold, taciturn mien served their silly souls as signs of wisdom and ability!

Of necessity dignities and offices are bestowed more by fortune than by merit: you often do wrong to blame kings for that. On the contrary, it is a wonder that they have such good luck, enjoying as they do so few ways of finding out.

Principis est virtus maxima nosse suos,

[For a prince, the chief merit is to know his subjects,][31]

for Nature has not given them eyes which can extend over so many peoples, distinguishing pre-eminence and seeing

30. Erasmus, *Apophthegmata*, VI, *Diversorum Graecorum*, XXXII.
31. Martial, *Epigrams*, VIII, 15.

into our bosoms, where is lodged the knowledge of our will and of our better qualities. They have to select us by fumbling guesses: by our family, our wealth, our learning and the voice of the people – the feeblest of arguments. Anyone who could discover the means by which men could be justly judged and reasonably chosen would, at a stroke, establish a perfect form of commonwealth.

'Yes. But he brought this great matter to a successful conclusion.' – That means something, but not enough; for we rightly accept the maxim which says that plans must not be judged by results. The Carthaginians punished bad counsels in their captains even when they were put right by a happy outcome. And the Roman people often refused to mark great and beneficial victories because the qualities of leadership of the commander were inferior to his good luck. In this world's activities we often notice that Fortune rivals Virtue: she shows us what power she has over everything and delights in striking down our presumption by making the incompetent lucky since she cannot make them wise. She loves to interfere, favouring those performances whose course has been entirely her own. That is why we can see, every day, the simplest among us bringing the greatest public and private tasks to successful conclusions.

Siramnes the Persian replied to those who were amazed that his enterprises turned out so badly, seeing that his projects were so wise, by saying that he alone was master of his projects while Fortune was mistress of the outcome of his enterprises: they too could make the same reply to explain the opposite tendency.[32]

Most of this world's events happen by themselves:

> *Fata viam inveniunt.*
>
> [The Fates find a way.][33]

The outcome often lends authority to the most inept leadership. Our intervention is virtually no more than a habit, the result of tradition and example rather than of reason. I was once astounded by the greatness of a venture; I then learnt from those who had brought it to a successful conclusion what their motives were and what methods they used: I found nothing but ordinary notions.

Indeed the most ordinary usual ones are also perhaps the most reliable and the most suitable in practice if not for show. What if the most lowly reasons are the most solidly based? What if the most humble, most lax and best-trodden ones are the most suited to our concerns? If we are to safeguard the authority of the Privy Council we do not need laymen participating in it nor seeing further

32. Cited by Amyot in his Prologue to *Les Vies de Plutarque*.
33. Virgil, *Aeneid*, III, 395; then, Horace, *Odes*, I, ix, 9.

than the first obstacle. If we want to maintain its reputation it must be taken on trust, as a whole.

My thought sketches out the matter for a while and dwells lightly on the first aspects of it: then I usually leave the principal thrust of the task to heaven.

Permitte divis cætera.

[Entrust the rest to the gods.]

To my mind Good Luck and Bad Luck are two sovereign powers. There is no wisdom in thinking that the role of Fortune can be played by human wisdom. What he undertakes is vain if a man should presume to embrace both causes and consequences and to lead the progress of his action by the hand; and it is especially vain in counsels of war. Never were there more military circumspection and prudence than I sometimes see practised among us:[34] perhaps we fear that we shall get lost en route, and therefore keep ourselves in reserve for the climax in the final act!

I will go on to say that our very wisdom and mature reflections are for the most part led by chance. My will and my reasoning are stirred this way and that. And many

---

34. '88: never were there *such* military circumspection and prudence, *especially in our nation* as I see practised: perhaps . . .

of their movements govern themselves without me. My reason is daily subject to incitements and agitations which are due to chance:

> *Vertuntur species animorum, et pectora motus*
> *Nunc alios, alios dum nubila ventus agebat,*
> *Concipiunt.*

[Their minds' ideas are ever turning round; the emotions in their breasts are driven hither and thither like clouds before the wind.][35]

Look and see who wield most power in our cities; who do their jobs best. You will find that they are usually the least clever. There have been cases when women, children and lunatics have ruled their states equally as well as the most talented princes. Coarse men more usually succeed in such things, says Thucydides, better than the subtle ones do.[36] We ascribe the deeds of their good fortune to their wisdom.

> *Ut quisque fortuna utitur*
> *Ita præcellet, atque exinde sapere illum omnes dicimus.*

[Each outstanding man is raised by his good fortune; we then say that he is clever.]

35. Virgil, *Georgics*, I, 420–22.
36. Thucydides, cited (with others of the above) from Justus Lipsius' *Politici*, as is the following, from Plautus' *Pseudolus*.

That is why I insist that, in all our activities, their outcomes provide meagre testimony of our worth and ability.

Now I was just about to say that it merely suffices for us to see a man raised to great dignity; even though we knew him three days before to be a negligible man, there seeps into our opinions, unawares, a notion of greatness, of talents, and we convince ourselves that by growing in style and reputation he has grown in merit. Our judgements of him are not based on his worth but (as is the case with the counters of an abacus) on the tokens of rank. Let his luck turn again, let him have a fall and be lost in the crowd again, then we all ask in wonder what had made him soar so high! 'Is this the same man?' we ask. 'Did he not know more about it when he was up there? Are princes satisfied with so little? We were in good hands, indeed we were!'

That is something I have seen many times in my own days.

Why, even the mask of greatness which is staged in our plays affects us somewhat and deceives us. What I worship in kings is the crowd of their worshippers. Everything should bow and submit to our kings – except our intelligence. My reason was not made for bending and bowing, my knees were.

When Melanthius was asked how Dionysius' tragedy

appeared to him, 'I never saw it,' he replied. 'It was obscured by the words!' So, too, most of those who judge what the great have to say ought to answer: 'I never heard his words: they were too much obscured by his dignity, grandeur and majesty.'[37]

One day, when Antisthenes urged the Athenians to command that donkeys be used, as their horses were, to plough their fields, he was told that donkeys were not born for such a service. 'That does not matter,' he retorted. 'It all depends on your issuing the order: for the most ignorant and incompetent men whom you put in command of your wars never fail to become suddenly most worthy of command, because it is you who employ them!'[38]

Related to this is the practice of so many people to sanctify the kings whom they have chosen from among themselves. They are not contented with honouring them: they need to worship them. The people of Mexico dare not look at the face of their king once they have completed the rites of his enthronement, but as though they had deified him by his royal state they make him swear not merely to maintain their religion, laws and liberties and to be valiant, just and debonair, he must also swear to cause the sun to run shining with its accustomed light, the

37. Plutarch (tr. Amyot), *Comment il faut ouïr*, 64 H.
38. Erasmus, *Apophthegmata*, VII, *Antisthenes*, XXX.

clouds to break in due season, the rivers to flow in their courses and the earth to bring forth all things needful for his people.[39]

I am opposed to that widespread fashion and I most doubt a man's ability when I see it accompanied by great rank and public acclaim. We should remember what it means to a man to be able to speak when he wants to, to choose the right moment, to break off the discussion or switch the subject with the authority of a master, to defend himself against objections with a shake of the head, a little smile or with silence, in front of courtiers who tremble with reverence and respect.

A monstrously rich man, when some trivial matter was being aired casually over dinner, joined in the discussion and began with these very words: 'Anyone who says otherwise is either ignorant or a liar,' and so on. You had better follow up that philosophical thrust with a dagger in your hand!

Here is another warning, which I find most useful: in debates and discussions we should not immediately be impressed by what we take to be a man's own *bons mots*. Most men are rich with other men's abilities. It may well be that such-and-such a man makes a fine remark, a good

39. Lopez de Gomara (tr. Fumée), *Histoire générale des Indes*, II, lxxvii.

reply or a pithy saying, advancing it without realizing its power. (That we do not grasp everything we borrow can doubtless be proved from my own case.) We should not always give way, no matter what beauty or truth it may have. We should either seriously attack it or else, under pretence of not understanding it, retreat a little so as to probe it thoroughly and to discover how it is lodged in its author. We may be helping his sword-thrust to carry beyond his reach, running on to it ourselves. There have been times when, pressed by necessity in the duel of words, I have made counter-attacks which struck home more than I ever hoped or expected. I was counting their number: they were accepted for their weight.

When I am disputing with a man of strong arguments I enjoy anticipating his conclusions; I save him the bother of explaining himself; I make an assay at forestalling his ideas while they are still unfinished and being formed (the order and stretch of his intelligence warn me and threaten me from afar). Similarly, with those others I mentioned I do quite the opposite: we should suppose nothing, understand nothing but what they explain. If their judgements are apposite but expressed in universals – 'This is good: that is bad' – find out whether it is luck which makes them apposite. Make them circumscribe and restrict their verdict a little: 'Why is it good? How is it good?' Those

universal judgements (which I find so common) say nothing. They are like those who greet people as a mass or a crowd: those who have genuine knowledge of them greet them by name and distinguish them as individuals.[40] But it is a chancy business. Which explains why, on average more than once a day, I have seen men with ill-founded minds trying to act clever by showing me some beautiful detail in the book they are reading, but choosing so badly the point on which they fix their admiration that instead of revealing the excellence of their author they reveal their own ignorance.

When you have just listened to a whole page of Virgil you can safely exclaim, 'Now that is beautiful!' The cunning ones escape that way. But to undertake to go back over the detail of a good author, to try to indicate with precise and selected examples where he surpasses himself and where he flies high by weighing his words and his locutions and his choice of materials one after another: not many try that. '*Videndum est non modo quid quisque loquatur, sed etiam quid quisque sentiat, atque etiam qua de causa quisque sentiat.*' [We should not only examine what each one says, but what are his opinions and what grounds he has for holding them.][41] Day after day I hear stupid people uttering words which are not stupid. They say something

40. Plutarch (tr. Amyot), *De l'esprit familier de Socrates*, 636 BC.
41. Cicero, *De officiis*, I, xli, 147.

good; let us discover how deeply they understand it and where they got hold of it. They do not own that fine saying or that fine reasoning, but we help them to use it. They are only looking after it. Perhaps they only produced it fortuitously, hesitantly: it is we who give it credit and value. You are lending them a hand. But why? They feel no gratitude towards you for it and become all the more silly. Do not support them; let them go their own way: they will handle that material like a man who fears getting scalded: they dare not show it in a different light or context nor to deepen it. Give it the tiniest shaking and it slips away from them: then, strong and beautiful though it be, they surrender it to you. They have beautiful weapons, but the handles are loose! How often have I learnt that from experience!

Now, if you come and clarify and reinforce it for them, they immediately take advantage of your interpretation and rob you of it: 'That is what I was about to say,' or, 'That is how I understand it, exactly,' or, 'If I did not put it that way it was because I could not find the right words.' – Bluster on! We should use even cunning to punish such arrogant stupidity.

Hegesias' principle that we should neither hate nor blame but instruct is right elsewhere but not here.[42]

42. Diogenes Laertius, *Life of Aristippus*.

There is neither justice nor kindness in helping a man to get up who does not know how to use your help and who is all the worse for it. I like to let them sink deeper in the mire and to get even more entangled – so deeply that, if possible, even they finally realize it!

You cannot cure silliness and unreasonableness by one act of warning. Of that sort of cure we can properly say what Cyrus replied to the man who urged him to give an exhortation to his troops at the moment of battle: that men are not made courageous warriors on the battlefield by a good harangue any more than you can become a good musician by hearing a good song.[43] Apprenticeships must be served, before you set hand to anything, by long and sustained study.

It is to our own folk that we owe this obligation to be assiduous in correcting and instructing; but to go preaching at the first passer-by or to read lectures on ignorance and silliness to the first man we come across is a practice which I loathe. I rarely do it during discussions in which I am involved; I prefer to let it all go by rather than to resort to such remote and donnish lecturing. My humour is unsuited, both in speaking and writing, to those who are learning first principles. But however false or absurd I

43. Xenophon, *Cyropaedia*, III, iii, 49–50.

judge things to be which are said in company or before a third party, I never leap in to interrupt them by word or gesture.

Meanwhile nothing in stupidity irritates me more than its being much more pleased with itself than any reasonableness could reasonably be. It is a disaster that wisdom forbids you to be satisfied with yourself and always sends you away dissatisfied and fearful, whereas stubbornness and foolhardiness fill their hosts with joy and assurance. It is the least clever of men who look down at others over their shoulders, always returning from the fray full of glory and joyfulness. And as often as not their haughty language and their happy faces win them victory in the eyes of the bystanders who are generally feeble in judging and incapable of discerning real superiority. The surest proof of animal-stupidity is ardent obstinacy of opinion. Is there anything more certain, decided, disdainful, contemplative, grave and serious, than a donkey?

Perhaps we may include in the category of conversation and discussion those short pointed exchanges which happiness and intimacy introduce among friends when pleasantly joking together and sharply mocking each other. That is a sport for which my natural gaiety makes me rather well-suited; and if it is not as tensely serious as the

other sport I have just described, it is no less keen and

clever, nor, as it seemed to Lycurgus, any less useful.[44] Where I am concerned I contribute more licence than wit, being more happy in that than in finding any material; but I am a perfect target, for I can put up with retaliation without getting angry not merely when sharp but even when rude. When I am suddenly attacked, if I cannot at once find a good repartee I do not waste time following up that thrust with vague boring contestations akin to stubbornness but I let it go by, cheerfully flapping down my ears and waiting for a better moment to get my own back. No huckster wins every haggle.

Most people, when their arguments fail, change voice and expression, and instead of retrieving themselves betray their weaknesses and susceptibility by an unmannerly anger. In the excitement of jesting we can sometimes nip those secret chords of one another's imperfections which we cannot even pluck without offence when we are calm; we warn each other profitably of each other's faults. There are other sports, physical ones, rash and harsh in the French manner, which I hate unto death. I am touchy and sensitive about such things: in my lifetime I have seen two princes of the blood royal laid in their

44. Perhaps a vague recollection of Plutarch (tr. Amyot), *Du trop parler*, 95 BC, or of Lycurgus' forbidding of hand-to-hand sports among citizens (Henry Estienne, *Apophthegmata*, 1568, pp. 416–17).

graves because of them. It is an ugly thing to fight for fun.[45]

In addition when I want to judge another man I ask him to what extent he is himself satisfied; how far he is happy with what he has said or written. I want him to avoid those fine excuses: 'I was only playing at it' –

Ablatum mediis opus est incudibus istud

[It was taken off the anvil only half finished][46]

– 'I only spent an hour on it'; 'I have not seen it since'. – 'All right,' I say: 'let us leave those examples. Show me something which does represent you entirely, something by which you are happy to be measured.' And then I say, 'What do you consider the most beautiful aspect of your work? Is it this quality or that quality? Is it its gracious style, its subject-matter, your discovery of the material, your judgement, your erudition?'

For I normally find that men are as wrong in judging their own work as other people's, not simply because their emotions are involved but because they lack the ability to understand it and to analyse it. The work itself, by its own

---

45. Henry II was killed while jousting; Henry, Marquess of Beaupréau died of wounds received in a tournament. There were other cases as well.

46. Ovid, *Tristia*, I, vii, 9.

momentum and fortune, can favour the author beyond his own understanding and research; it can run ahead of him. There is no work that I can judge with less certainty than my own: the *Essays* I place – very hesitantly and with little assurance – sometimes low, sometimes high.

Many books are useful for their subject-matter: their authors derive little glory from them. And there are good books which as far as good workmanship is concerned are a disgrace to their authors. I could write about our style of feasting, about our clothing – and I could write it gracelessly; I could publish contemporary edicts and the letters of princes which come into the public domain; I could make an abridgement of a good book (and every abridgement of a good book is a daft one) and then the book itself could chance to get lost. Things like that. From such compilations posterity would derive unique assistance: but what honour would I derive from them except for being lucky? A good proportion of famous books fall in that category.

When I was reading a few years ago Philippe de Commines – a very good author, certainly – I noted the following saying as being above average: 'We should be wary of doing such great services to our master that we render him unable to reward them justly.' I should have praised not him but his discovery of a topic. Not long ago I came upon this sentence in Tacitus: '*Beneficia eo usque læta sunt dum videntur exolvi posse; ubi multum antevenere, pro gratia odium redditur.'* [Good turns are pleasing only in so far as they seem repayable. Much beyond that we repay with hatred not gratitude.] Seneca puts it forcefully: *'Nam qui putat esse turpe non reddere, non vult esse cui reddat.'* [He for whom not to repay is a disgrace wants his benefactor dead.] Quintus Cicero, with a laxer turn of phrase, writes: *'Qui se non putat satisfacere, amicus esse nullo modo potest.'* [He who cannot repay his debt to you can in no wise love you.][47]

An author's subject can, when appropriate, show him to be erudite or retentive, but if you are to judge what qualities in him most truly belong to him and are the most honourable (I mean the force and beauty of his soul) you must know what is really his and what definitely is not; and in that which is not, how much we are indebted to him for his selection, disposition, ornamentation and the literary quality of what he had contributed. Supposing he has taken somebody else's matter and then ruined the style, as often happens! People like us who have little experience of books are in difficulties when we come

47. Montaigne is contrasting *inventio* (the discovery of arguments or topics) with original powers of judgement. Philippe de Commines, III, xii; Tacitus, *Annals*, IV, xviii; Seneca, *Epist. moral.*, LXXXVI, 32; Cicero, *De petitione consultatus*, ix.

across some fine example of ingenuity in a modern poet or some strong argument in a preacher. We dare not praise them for it before we have learned from a scholar whether that item is original to them or taken from another. Until I have done that I remain suspicious.

I have just read through at one go Tacitus' *History* (something which rarely happens to me: it is twenty years since I spent one full hour at a time on a book. I did it on the recommendation of a nobleman highly esteemed in France both for his own virtue and for that sustained quality of ability and goodness which he is seen to share with his many brothers). I know of no author who combines a chronicle of public events with so much reflection on individual morals and biases.[48] And it appears to me (contrary to what appears to him) that, as he has the particular task of following the careers of the contemporary Emperors (men so odd and so extreme in their various characters) as well as the noteworthy deeds which they provoked in their subjects above all by their cruelty, he has a more striking and interesting topic to relate and discourse upon than if he had to tell of battles and world revolutions. Consequently I find him unprofitable when he dashes through those fair, noble deaths as though he

48. '88: biases. *In that he is no less careful and diligent than Plutarch, who made an express claim to do so.* This manner . . .

were afraid of tiring us by accounts both too long and too numerous.

This manner of history is by far the most useful. The unrolling of public events depends more on the guiding hand of Fortune: that of private ones, on our own.[49] Tacitus' work is more a judgement on historical events than a narration of them. There are more precepts than accounts. It is not a book to be read but one to be studied and learnt. It is so full of aphorisms that, apposite or not, they are everywhere. It is a seed-bed of ethical and political arguments to supply and adorn those who hold high rank in the governing of this world. He pleads his case with solid and vigorous reasons, in an epigrammatic and exquisite style following the affected manner of his century. (They were so fond of a high style that when they found no wit or subtlety in their subject-matter they resorted to witty subtle words.) He is not all that different from Seneca, but while he seems to have more flesh on him Seneca is more acute. Tacitus can more properly serve a sickly troubled nation like our own is at present: you could often believe that we were the subject of his narrating and berating. Those who doubt his good faith clearly betray that they resent him from prejudice. He has

49. '88: our own. *Yet he did not overlook what he owed to the other aspect.* Tacitus' work . . .

sound opinions and inclines to the right side in the affairs of Rome. I do regret though that, by making Pompey no better than Marius and Scylla only more secretive, he judged him more harshly than is suggested by the verdict of men who lived and dealt with him.[50] True, Pompey's striving to govern affairs has not been cleared of ambition nor a wish for vengeance: even his friends feared that victory might make him go out of his mind, though not to the extremes of insanity of those other two. Nothing in his life suggests to us the menace of such express tyranny and cruelty. Besides we ought never to let suspicions outweigh evidence: so on this point I do not trust Tacitus.

That the accounts which he gives are indeed simple and straight can perhaps be argued from the very fact that they do not exactly fit his concluding judgements, to which he is led by the slant he had adopted; they often go beyond the evidence which he provides – which he had not deigned to bias in the slightest degree. He needs no defence for having assented to the religion of his day, in accordance with the laws which bade him to do so, and for being ignorant of the true religion. That is his misfortune not his fault.[51]

50. Tacitus, *Histories*, II, xxxviii.
51. Once more a judgement *secundum quid* (in this case according to the standard of the laws of Tacitus' day). It was not Tacitus' fault,

What I have chiefly been considering is his judgement: I am not entirely clear about it. For example, take these words from the letter sent to the Senate by the aged ailing Tiberius: 'What, Sirs, should I write to you, what indeed should I not write to you at this time? I know that I am daily nearing death; may the gods and goddesses make my end worse if I know what to write.' I cannot see why he applies them with such certainty to a poignant remorse tormenting Tiberius' conscience. Leastways when I came across them I saw no such thing.[52]

It also seemed to me a bit weak of him when he was obliged to mention that he had once held an honourable magistracy in Rome to go on and explain that he was not referring to it in order to boast about it. That line seemed rather shoddy to me for a soul such as his: not to dare to talk roundly of yourself betrays a defect of thought. A man of straight and elevated mind who judges surely and soundly employs in all circumstances examples taken from himself as well as from others, and frankly cites himself as witness as well as third parties. We should jump over those plebeian rules of etiquette in favour of truth and freedom. I not only dare to talk about myself but to talk

---

since a knowledge of Christian truth requires prevenient grace, which by definition cannot be in any way earned or deserved.

52. Tacitus, *Annals*, VI, vi.

of nothing but myself. I am wandering off the point when I write of anything else, cheating my subject of *me*. I do not love myself with such lack of discretion, nor am I so bound and involved in myself, that I am unable to see myself apart and to consider myself separately as I would a neighbour or a tree. The error is the same if you fail to see the limits of your worth or if you report more than you can see. We owe more love to God than to ourselves.[53] We know him less, yet talk about him till we are glutted.

If Tacitus' writings tell us anything at all about his character, he was a very great man, upright and courageous, whose virtue was not of the superstitious kind but philosophical and magnanimous. You could find some of his testimony rather rash; for example he maintains that when a soldier's hands grew stiff with the cold while carrying a pile of wood they adhered to his load, broke away from his arms and stuck there dead.[54] In similar cases my custom is to bow to the authority of such great witnesses. When he says that, by favour of Serapis the

---

53. Montaigne apparently accepts the contention of Duns Scotus (and others) that when a man loves himself or any other creature properly he loves God even more. Luther and many others denied this (*Weimarer Ausgabe*, XL, p. 461). Montaigne's contention is more traditionally Catholic than Humanist.

54. Tacitus, *Annals*, XIII, xxxv; then, IV, lxxi (seen by some as a parody of Christ's curing the blind man in Mark 8:23).

god, Vespasian cured a blind woman in Alexandria by anointing her eyes with his saliva and also performed some additional miracle or other, he was following the dutiful example of all good historians who keep a chronicle of important happenings: included among public events are popular rumours and opinions. Their role is to give an account of popular beliefs, not to account for them: which part is played by Theologians and philosophers as directors of consciences. That is why his fellow-historian, great man as he was, most wisely said: '*Equidem plura transcribo quam credo: nam nec affirmare sustineo, de quibus dubito, nec subducere quae accepi.*' [I do indeed pass on more than I believe. I cannot vouch for the things which I doubt, nor can I omit what I have been told by tradition.] And another says: '*Haec neque affirmare, neque refellere operae pretium est: famae rerum standum est.*' [These things are neither to be vouched for nor denied: we must cling to tradition.][55] Tacitus, writing during a period in which belief in portents was on the wane, says that he nevertheless does not wish to fail to provide a foothold for them, and so includes in his *Annals* matters accepted by so many decent people with so great a reverence for antiquity.

That is very well said. Let them pass on their histories to us according to what they find received, not according

55. Quintus Curtius, IX, i; Livy, VIII, vi.

to their own estimate. I, who am monarch of the subject which I treat and not accountable for it to anyone, do not for all that believe everything I say. Sometimes my mind launches out with paradoxes which I mistrust and with verbal subtleties which make me shake my head; but I let them take their chance. I know that some men gain a reputation from such things. It is not for me alone to judge them. I describe myself standing up and lying down, from front and back, from right and left and with all my inborn complexities. Even minds[56] of sustained power are not always sustained in their application and discernment.

That is, *grosso modo*, the Tacitus which is presented to me, vaguely enough, by my memory. All *grosso-modo* judgements are lax and defective.[57]

---

56. '88: even *judgements* which are . . .
57. '88: All *universal* judgements are lax and *dangerous* . . .

On Thumbs

[Renaissance etymologies are often very fanciful, but in the case of the French and Latin words for thumb (pouce, pollex) philologists today continue to accept the derivations advanced by Montaigne and his contemporaries. Our own word 'thumb' derives also, it seems, from a Sanskrit word meaning 'the strong one'.]

Tacitus relates that it was the custom among certain Barbarian kings to make a treaty binding by pressing their right hands together and interlocking their thumbs until they had squeezed the blood to their tips, whereupon they lightly pricked them with a needle and sucked each other's blood.[1]

Doctors say that our thumb is our master-finger and that our French word for it, *pouce*, derives from the Latin verb *pollere* [to excel in strength].[2] The Greeks called it *anticheir*, 'another hand', so to speak. And the Latins

---

1. Tacitus, *Annals*, XII, xlvii.
2. *Pollex*, the Latin for thumb, 'the strong one', was indeed derived from the verb 'to be strong'. Cf. Macrobius, *Saturnalia*, VII, xiii. The Greek etymology is fanciful.

seem occasionally to use it to mean the whole of the hand:

> *Sed nec vocibus excitata blandis,*
> *Molli pollice nec rogata, surgit.*

[Neither sweet words of persuasion nor the help of
her thumb can get it erect.]

In Rome it was a sign of approval to turn your thumbs
and twist them downwards –

> *Fautor utroque tuum laudabit pollice ludum*

[Your fans admire your play by turning down
both their thumbs]

– and of disapproval to raise them and extend them
outwards:

> *converso pollice vulgi*
> *Quemlibet occidunt populariter.*

[when the mob twist their thumbs round, anyone
at all is slaughtered to their acclaim.][3]

3. Martial, *Epigrams*, XII, xcviii, 8; Horace, *Epist.*, I, xviii, 66;
Juvenal, III, 36. (Our 'thumbs up' was 'thumbs down' for the
Romans.)

The Romans exempted from war service those who had injured thumbs since they could no longer firmly grasp their weapons. Augustus confiscated the estates of a Roman knight who had craftily cut off the thumb of two of his sons to stop them being mobilized into the army. Before that, during the Italian Wars, the Senate had sentenced Caius Vatienus to life imprisonment and confiscated all his estates for having deliberately cut off his left thumb to get out of an expedition. Some general or other (I cannot remember his name) cut off the thumb of his defeated enemies after winning a naval engagement so as to deprive them of the means of fighting and of pulling on the oar.[4] The Athenians did the same to the men of Aegina to deprive them of their naval superiority.[5] In Sparta the schoolmaster punished his pupils by biting their thumbs.

4. Suetonius, *Augustus*, XXIV; Valerius Maximus, V; Plutarch, *Life of Lysander*. Philoctetes left them *able* to row (in the galleys).

5. Cicero, *De officiis*, III, xi, 46; then, Plutarch, *Life of Lysander*.

PENGUIN 60s

are published on the occasion of Penguin's 60th anniversary

LOUISA MAY ALCOTT · *An Old-Fashioned Thanksgiving and Other Stories*

HANS CHRISTIAN ANDERSEN · *The Emperor's New Clothes*

J. M. BARRIE · *Peter Pan in Kensington Gardens*

WILLIAM BLAKE · *Songs of Innocence and Experience*

GEOFFREY CHAUCER · *The Wife of Bath and Other Canterbury Tales*

ANTON CHEKHOV · *The Black Monk* and *Peasants*

SAMUEL TAYLOR COLERIDGE · *The Rime of the Ancient Mariner*

COLETTE · *Gigi*

JOSEPH CONRAD · *Youth*

ROALD DAHL · *Lamb to the Slaughter and Other Stories*

ROBERTSON DAVIES · *A Gathering of Ghost Stories*

FYODOR DOSTOYEVSKY · *The Grand Inquisitor*

SIR ARTHUR CONAN DOYLE · *The Man with the Twisted Lip*
    and *The Adventure of the Devil's Foot*

RALPH WALDO EMERSON · *Nature*

OMER ENGLEBERT (TRANS.) · *The Lives of the Saints*

FANNIE FARMER · *The Original 1896 Boston Cooking-School Cook Book*

EDWARD FITZGERALD (TRANS.) · *The Rubáiyát of Omar Khayyám*

ROBERT FROST · *The Road Not Taken and Other Early Poems*

GABRIEL GARCÍA MÁRQUEZ · *Bon Voyage, Mr President and Other Stories*

NIKOLAI GOGOL · *The Overcoat* and *The Nose*

GRAHAM GREENE · *Under the Garden*

JACOB AND WILHELM GRIMM · *Grimm's Fairy Tales*

NATHANIEL HAWTHORNE · *Young Goodman Brown and Other Stories*

O. HENRY · *The Gift of the Magi and Other Stories*

WASHINGTON IRVING · *Rip Van Winkle* and *The Legend of Sleepy Hollow*

HENRY JAMES · *Daisy Miller*

V. S. VERNON JONES (TRANS.) · *Aesop's Fables*

JAMES JOYCE · *The Dead*

GARRISON KEILLOR · *Truckstop and Other Lake Wobegon Stories*

JACK KEROUAC · *San Francisco Blues*
STEPHEN KING · *Umney's Last Case*
RUDYARD KIPLING · *Baa Baa, Black Sheep* and *The Gardener*
LAO TZU · *Tao Te Ching*
D. H. LAWRENCE · *Love Among the Haystacks*
ABRAHAM LINCOLN · *The Gettysburg Address and Other Speeches*
JACK LONDON · *To Build a Fire and Other Stories*
HERMAN MELVILLE · *Bartleby* and *The Lightning-rod Man*
A. A. MILNE · *Winnie-the-Pooh and His Friends*
MICHEL DE MONTAIGNE · *Four Essays*
JOHN MORTIMER · *Rumpole and the Younger Generation*
THOMAS PAINE · *The Crisis*
DOROTHY PARKER · *Big Blonde and Other Stories*
EDGAR ALLAN POE · *The Pit and the Pendulum and Other Stories*
EDGAR ALLAN POE, AMBROSE BIERCE,
    AND ROBERT LOUIS STEVENSON · *Three Tales of Horror*
FRANKLIN DELANO ROOSEVELT · *Fireside Chats*
WILLIAM SHAKESPEARE · *Sixty Sonnets*
JOHN STEINBECK · *The Chrysanthemums and Other Stories*
PETER STRAUB · *Blue Rose*
PAUL THEROUX · *The Greenest Island*
HENRY DAVID THOREAU · *Walking*
JOHN THORN · *Baseball: Our Game*
LEO TOLSTOY · *Master and Man*
MARK TWAIN · *The Notorious Jumping Frog of Calaveras County*
H. G. WELLS · *The Time Machine*
EDITH WHARTON · *Madame de Treymes*
OSCAR WILDE · *The Happy Prince and Other Stories*
The Declaration of Independence and *The Constitution of the United States*
Mother Goose
The Revelation of St. John the Divine
Teachings of Jesus

FOR THE BEST IN PAPERBACKS, LOOK FOR THE

In every corner of the world, on every subject under the sun, Penguin represents quality and variety—the very best in publishing today.

For complete information about books available from Penguin—including Puffins, Penguin Classics, and Arkana—and how to order them, write to us at the appropriate address below. Please note that for copyright reasons the selection of books varies from country to country.